With love and thanks to my family
for the memories of Christmas past,
the joys of Christmas present, and
the promise of Christmas yet-to-come.

A CUP OF CHRISTMAS TEA
Mary Ellen Enterprises
6414 Cambridge Street
St. Louis Park, MN 55426-4461
Copyright ©1981 by Tom Hegg & Warren Hanson
ALL RIGHTS RESERVED
ISBN: 0-941298-08-6
Printed in the United States of America
Second Printing:
10   9   8   7   6   5   4   3   2

A Cup of Christmas Tea

by Tom Hegg

illustrated by Warren Hanson

*The log was in the fireplace,
all spiced and set to burn.*

At last, the yearly Christmas race
        was in the clubhouse turn.
The cards were in the mail,
        all the gifts beneath the tree,
And 30 days reprieve
        'till VISA could catch up with me.

And though smug satisfaction
      seemed the order of the day,
Something still was nagging me,
      and would not go away.
A week before, I got a letter
      from my old Great Aunt.
It read: "Of course, I'll understand
      completely if you can't,
But if you find you have some time,
      how wonderful if we
Could have a little chat
      and share a cup of Christmas tea."

She'd had a mild stroke that year
     which crippled her left side.
Though housebound now, my folks had said
     it hadn't hurt her pride.
They said: "She'd love to see you.
     What a nice thing it would be
For you to go and maybe
     have a cup of Christmas tea."

But boy! I didn't want to go!
     Oh, what a bitter pill
To see an old relation
     and how far she'd gone downhill.
I remembered her as vigorous,
     as funny and as bright.
I remembered Christmas Eves
     when she regaled us half the night.
I didn't want to risk all that.
     I didn't want the pain.

I didn't need to be depressed.
   I didn't need the strain.
And what about my brother?
   Why not him? She's his Aunt, too!
I thought I had it justified,
   but then before I knew,
The reasons not to go
   I so painstakingly had built
Were cracking wide and crumbling
   in an acid rain of guilt.

I put on boots and gloves and cap,
shame stinging every pore,
And armed with squeegee, sand and map,
I went out my front door.

I drove in from the suburbs
        to the older part of town.
The pastels of the newer homes
        gave way to gray and brown.

I had that disembodied feeling
as the car pulled up
And stopped beside the wooden house
that held the Christmas cup.
How I got up to her door,
I really couldn't tell...

I watched my hand rise up
          and press the button of the bell.

I waited,
          aided by my nervous rocking to and fro,
And just as I was thinking
          I should turn around and go,
I heard the rattle of the china
          in the hutch against the wall.
The triple beat of two feet and a crutch
          came down the hall.

The clicking of the door latch
    and the sliding of the bolt,
And a little swollen struggle
    popped it open with a jolt.

She stood there, pale and tiny,
*   looking fragile as an egg...*
I forced myself from staring at the brace
*   that held her leg.*
And though her thick bifocals
*   seemed to crack and spread her eyes,*
Their milky and refracted depths
*   lit up with young surprise.*

"Come in! Come in!" She laughed the words.
She took me by the hand,
And all my fears dissolved away,
as if by her command.
We went inside, and then,
before I knew how to react,

Before my eyes and ears and nose
  was Christmas past...alive...intact.

The scent of candied oranges,
of cinnamon and pine
The antique wooden soldiers
in their military line;

The porcelain Nativity
     I'd always loved so much...
The Dresden and the crystal
     I'd been told I mustn't touch...

My spirit fairly bolted,
*   like a child out of class*
And danced among the ornaments
*   of calico and glass.*
Like magic, I was six again,
*   deep in a Christmas spell,*
Steeped in the million memories
*   the boy inside knew well.*

And here, among old Christmas cards,
so lovingly displayed,
A special place of honor
for the ones we kids had made.

And there, beside her rocking chair,
       the center of it all...
My Great Aunt stood and said
        how nice it was I'd come to call.

I sat...and rattled on about...
        the weather and the flu.
She listened very patiently,
        then smiled and said, "What's new?"
Thoughts and words began to flow.
        I started making sense.
I lost the phoney breeziness
        I use when I get tense.
She was still passionately interested
        in everything I did.
She was positive. Encouraging.
        Like when I was a kid.

Simple generalities
          still sent her into fits.
She demanded the specifics.
          The particulars. The bits.
We talked about the limitations
          that she'd had to face.
She spoke with utter candor,
          and with humor and good grace.
Then, defying the reality
          of crutch and straightened knee,
On wings of hospitality,
          she flew to brew the tea.

I sat alone with feelings
that I hadn't felt in years.
I looked around at Christmas
through a thick, hot blur of tears.
And the candles and the holly
she'd arranged on every shelf...
The impossibly good cookies
she still somehow baked herself...

But these rich, tactile memories
       became quite pale and thin
When measured by the Christmas
       my Great Aunt kept deep within.
Her body halved and nearly spent,
       but my Great Aunt was whole.
I saw a Christmas miracle...
       the triumph of a soul.

The triple beat of two feet and a crutch
      came down the hall.
The rattle of the china
      in the hutch against the wall.
She poured two cups. She smiled,
      and then she handed one to me,

And then, we settled back
and had a cup of Christmas tea.

Acknowledgements:

Mr. Brian Anderson
Dr. & Mrs. Edward D. Berryman
Mr. David Dole
Mr. John Clark Donahue
Mr. Jules Ebin
Miss JoAnne Ferris
Miss Helen Hayes
Miss Elizabeth Heller
Mr. Roland Hill
Mr. William F. Lund
Dr. & Mrs. Donald M. Meisel
Miss Toni Mendez
Mr. Dave Moore

Mr. By Napier
Miss Frances A. Nelson
Mr. Peter MacNicol
Mr. & Mrs. Bill Rolland
Miss Maureen Ryan
Mr. Eddie Schwartz
Miss Allyn Sitjar
Miss Mara Ann Tapp
Miss Abigail Van Buren
Mr. Howard Viken
Dr. & Mrs. Dave Wood

My deepest gratitude for your love, encouragement and support.